Original title:

Burnished Icons Among the Ashen Thicket

Author: Mirell Mesipuu

ISBN HARDBACK: 978-1-80559-048-4

ISBN PAPERBACK: 978-1-80559-547-2

Shards of Light in the Whispering Wilds

In quiet glades where shadows play,
Small beams of hope begin to stray.
Through tangled vines and whispering trees,
Life stirs gently, carried by the breeze.

Mossy carpets beneath our feet,
Nature's pulse, a steady beat.
With every step, the world takes flight,
As blissful songs greet shards of light.

Among the ferns, a secret gleam,
A hidden brook, a silver stream.
Echoes dance in soft delight,
While stars emerge to bless the night.

Enchanting scents fill the air,
A tapestry of rich despair.
But in the wild's embracing hold,
Shards of light weave stories bold.

So linger here, where magic thrives,
In tranquil realms where wonder dives.
The whispering wilds, a gentle guide,
To shards of souls where dreams abide.

Silken Flames Amid Ashen Dreams

In twilight's grasp, emotions rise,
Silken flames in darkened skies.
Against the gray of fading day,
Hope flickers soft, then drifts away.

Ashen dreams on whispered air,
Fragmented wishes, none to spare.
Yet in the charred and muted night,
Silken flames begin to fight.

They shimmer bright, defying fate,
A dance of pasts we can't negate.
Gold and crimson in shades embrace,
Amidst the ash, we find our place.

With every spark, a story told,
Of lost desires and hearts grown bold.
In shadows cast by time's cruel beam,
We stoke the fires of our dreams.

So let the night envelop all,
In silken flames, we will not fall.
For ash may cloak what once was bright,
But deep within, we hold the light.

Faces of Light in Smoke-Draped Woods

Amidst the gray where shadows creep,
Soft whispers of the forest weep.
Flickering sparks break through the gloom,
Dancing like dreams in the dusky room.

Silent secrets drift on air,
Ghosts of woodlands, tall and fair.
Every flicker a tale unfolds,
Of ancient paths through leaves of gold.

The fragrance of pine, a lingering lie,
Guides wandering souls as they sigh.
Faces of light in the smoky veil,
Guide us through where shadows prevail.

Glimmering Flights Amidst the Ashfall

In the quiet where embers glow,
Wings of dreams begin to flow.
Glimmers flicker through the dusk,
A soft reminder, a hidden musk.

Ashfalls whisper of times gone by,
Echoes of laughter in the sky.
Each flight a memory, lost in time,
Rising to heights, a silent rhyme.

Through the ashes, colors blend,
A journey woven without end.
Glimmering flights in the dusky light,
Carry the past into the night.

Echoes of Flame Beneath the Shadowed Bough

Beneath the boughs of ancient trees,
Where whispers dance on gentle breeze.
Echoes of flame flicker bright,
Illuminating stories of the night.

Fires once roaring now only glow,
Memories linger in the flow.
Flickering light on bark and leaf,
Spins tales of joy, of loss, of grief.

In this embrace of wood and fire,
Hearts ignite with lost desire.
Echoes of flame breathe through the dark,
Guided by the eternal spark.

Radiant Traces in the Forgotten Thicket

In the thicket where shadows blend,
Radiant traces reach without end.
Whispers of light in a hidden glade,
Speak of the dreams that never fade.

Lost among brambles, time stands still,
Moments caught like a thrilling thrill.
Faint glimmers dance on dew-kissed grass,
Tracing the paths that shadows amass.

In this sanctuary, quiet and deep,
Nature's secrets softly creep.
Radiant traces that softly glow,
Guide the heart where few may go.

A Blaze of Glitter in the Tattered Wilderness

Amidst the trees, the sparkles dance,
A wild romance in nature's trance.
Beneath the sun, the shadows play,
In golden hues, the night meets day.

The whispers float on gentle breeze,
With vibrant colors, hearts to please.
Each step a treasure, new and bright,
In tattered wilds, we seek the light.

A blaze of hope that lights the way,
In tangled paths where wild things sway.
The glitter sings in every glance,
Inviting all to join the dance.

Through hands of time, the seasons change,
Yet through the chaos, paths arrange.
A symphony of life untold,
In wilderness, our dreams unfold.

So take a breath, find magic near,
With every glance, let go your fear.
For in this place, so wildly grand,
A blaze of glitter ever stands.

Shining Notes from the Heart of Ash

In silence deep, the embers glow,
From ashes rise, the spirits flow.
Each note a whisper, soft and clear,
A song of hope for all to hear.

Through burnt remains, new life will sprout,
In shadows deep, we find a route.
The heart of ash holds stories vast,
Of love and loss, both present and past.

Shining notes drift through the night,
With every chord, we seek the light.
In darkest times, the melodies soar,
A symphony that heals the sore.

The dance of flames, a fleeting glance,
With every flicker, souls entrance.
From scattered pieces, we create,
A harmony to celebrate.

So gather 'round, let voices rise,
In every note, the spirit flies.
For from the heart where ashes lay,
Shining notes will guide our way.

Sparkling Paths Across the Blackened Soil

In fields of dark where shadows cling,
A sparkle bright, a promise brings.
With every step, a chance to find,
The remnants of what love designed.

Across the soil, once filled with pain,
Now glimmers soft, like summer rain.
The past may haunt, but we must tread,
On paths of light where hope is fed.

Each footprint leaves a tale behind,
Of battles fought and hearts entwined.
The sparkling rays through ash and dust,
Illuminate our stride with trust.

Through blackened lands, the flowers bloom,
With colors bright, dispelling gloom.
A world reborn from what we sow,
In every heart, new strength will grow.

So let us walk with hearts anew,
On sparkling paths, both brave and true.
For in each step, we reignite,
The beauty born from darkest night.

Fragments of Light in a Sea of Soot

Amidst the gray where shadows merge,
Fragments of light begin to surge.
In every corner, hope is found,
A subtle shift in barren ground.

With every breath, we seek the flame,
In soot and ash, we dare reclaim.
The glimmers rise like stars on high,
A tapestry against the sky.

In tangled dreams where silence hums,
Resilience speaks, and courage comes.
Each fragment shines a path to take,
In darkest nights, awake, awake.

Through trials faced, the spirit bends,
Yet from these depths, the journey mends.
With every shard of sweet delight,
We weave a world of purest light.

So hold these pieces, wide and near,
In every heart, the sparks appear.
For in the sea of soot we stand,
Fragments of light, a guiding hand.

Embers of Forgotten Glory

In twilight's embrace, whispers sigh,
Faded tales of days gone by.
Ghostly echoes dance in the air,
A once-bright kingdom lost to despair.

Beneath the ashes, memories lie,
Time holds secrets it won't deny.
Dreams once golden, now dimmed and cold,
Flicker softly in shadows old.

Fragments of laughter, sweet and rare,
Haunt the ruins with tender care.
A crown of thorns rests upon the crown,
As hope withers and smiles drown.

A melody drifts through the night,
Carried on winds, distant and slight.
The embers flicker, refuse to fade,
In hearts where the light once played.

Yet deep in the silence, embers glow,
A spark of life, a chance to grow.
From forgotten glory, new flames arise,
Igniting the courage to touch the skies.

Shimmering Shadows in the Gloom

In the stillness, shadows weave,
Patterns soft as dreams believe.
Flickers dance on walls of night,
Whispered secrets bathed in light.

A silver sheen on leaves aglow,
Nature's breath, a gentle flow.
In every shimmer, a story told,
Of hidden treasures, bright and bold.

Murmurs of hope in every breeze,
Carrying tales through ancient trees.
The gloom softens, a tender shroud,
Where joy lives quietly, far from the crowd.

As darkness drapes the earth in care,
Shadows dance, a solemn prayer.
Echoes twinkling, a night's embrace,
In shimmering veils, we find our place.

Glint of the Lost Radiance

Beneath the earth, where silence reigns,
Lies a glimmer of forgotten chains.
Fleeting glimpses through cracks emerge,
A flickering pulse, a distant urge.

Once vibrant light that filled the skies,
Now buried deep, where memory lies.
Shadows stretch in the waning day,
Calling back the light, come what may.

Glimmers faint in the twilight's breath,
A heartbeat lingering, defying death.
The world above spins, unaware,
Of the glint of hope hidden in despair.

Tread softly upon this sacred ground,
Where echoes of brilliance can still be found.
With every step, the spirits rise,
Awakening the stars in our eyes.

Shattered Visions in Charred Woods

In charred remains where shadows grow,
Silent stories begin to flow.
Branches broken, hearts laid bare,
Whispers echo through the air.

Once, these woods held vibrant light,
Now they speak of pain and plight.
Fragments of dreams, scattered wide,
A haunting truth we cannot hide.

Amidst the ruins, life still stirs,
Resilience found in creatures' purrs.
Nature's canvas, raw and real,
Healing slowly, secrets conceal.

The winds carry tales of the past,
Of beauty lost, yet shadows cast.
In shattered visions, hope takes flight,
As dawn's embrace chases the night.

New beginnings from ashes rise,
A testament that never dies.
In charred woods, where life seems thin,
Rebirth ignites from within.

Gilded Shadows in the Charred Grove

In the charred grove shadows sway,
Whispering tales from yesterday.
Gilded leaves catch the fading light,
Where dreams once soared, now takes flight.

Amidst the ash, a new life grows,
From whispering winds, a story flows.
Silent echoes of love and grace,
Find their home, a gentle embrace.

Sunset dances on blackened trees,
Breath of hope in the wandering breeze.
As twilight dims the vibrant hue,
Stars awaken, draped in dew.

In shadows, the glimmers glint and shine,
History's scars begin to intertwine.
Gilded moments etched in time,
In the heart of darkness, life will climb.

With every heartbeat, courage ignites,
Casting warmth on the coldest nights.
In the grove where the past collides,
Gilded shadows become our guides.

Resilience of Radiance Amidst the Ruins

Among the ruins, light prevails,
In shattered dreams, a tale unveils.
Resilience blooms where hope is thin,
Radiance glows from deep within.

Each broken stone, a chapter wrought,
In the silence, wisdom sought.
Through fractured paths, the soul does tread,
In the darkest corners, stars are bred.

Time's soft hand weaves threads of gold,
In the tapestry of stories told.
Amidst the wreckage, beauty thrives,
With every heartbeat, spirit arrives.

Echoes of laughter fill the air,
Transforming despair into a prayer.
Resilience stands, unwavering, bold,
In the face of ruins, dreams unfold.

So raise your eyes to the limitless sky,
Let the past fade, let your spirit fly.
For even in loss, the heart finds peace,
In the steadfast glow, pain will cease.

Luminous Memories Beneath the Soot

Beneath the soot, memories gleam,
Each shadow holds a wistful dream.
Luminous echoes of laughter ring,
Whispers of joy that the heart will sing.

In the ashes, stories entwine,
Fragments of life, moments divine.
Through the darkness, the past endures,
In every heartbeat, the spirit cures.

Embers of friendship flicker bright,
Guiding us through the velvet night.
Luminous threads spun from the past,
Binding our souls, forever to last.

The weight of sorrow, a gentle caress,
In the quiet, we find our rest.
Beneath the soot, we rise anew,
With luminous courage to see us through.

As dawn approaches, hope reclaims,
Each memory shining, whispering names.
In the tapestry woven from time's embrace,
Luminous memories transcend space.

Shimmering Fragments of a Forgotten Fire

In the quiet dusk, embers glow,
Shimmering fragments of tales we know.
Forgotten fire whispers in the wind,
Carrying hopes where dreams have been.

The flicker of light through trees does dance,
In shadows cast, we take our chance.
With every spark, a story unfolds,
In the heart of darkness, warmth beholds.

Dusty paths where the wildflowers play,
Resilient spirits in shades of gray.
Shimmering remnants of moments dear,
Calling to hearts, drawing them near.

In the silence, echoes rise and swell,
Tales of wonder, a timeless spell.
Forgotten fire, a flicker's embrace,
In shimmering fragments, we find our place.

So gather around, let the stories ignite,
In the warmth of memory, take flight.
For within the ashes, a spark will remain,
Shimmering fragments of joy and pain.

Whispered Myths in Cinders and Smoke

In shadows deep, tales softly weave,
Of ancient dreams that none believe.
Flickering flames dance with the night,
Whispers echo, taking flight.

Ashen echoes of long-lost lore,
Secret voices, forevermore.
Beneath the layers, truth entwined,
In every ember, stories bind.

Figures form in the glowing haze,
Specters trapped in a smoky maze.
Each flicker, a moment, a thread,
In the cinders, all they said.

Lost legends of fire-touched dreams,
Rippling through like sunlit streams.
With every spark, new myths arise,
In the smoke, the ancient lies.

So gather close, let silence reign,
Feel the stories, bear the pain.
In whispered myths, we find a spark,
Kindling light in the deepest dark.

Glimmers of the Past in Scorched Earth

From ashes hushed, a tale unfolds,
Of distant lands and treasures bold.
Cracked earth whispers of days gone by,
As faded colors kiss the sky.

Through barren fields, the echoes roam,
Remnants point to a lost home.
In silence lingers the past's soft breath,
Telling stories of love and death.

Beneath the soil, memories sigh,
Waiting for the rains to cry.
Glimmers glint where shadows fall,
Hints of glory, echoes call.

The wind carries the songs of old,
Tales of heroes, brave and bold.
In every scar, a truth engraved,
In scorched earth, the past has braved.

So in your heart, let memories dwell,
In every tale, a fragile spell.
Embrace the glimmers, find the worth,
Of what remains in scorched earth.

Aglow in the Midnight Forest

In the forest where shadows creep,
Aglow with secrets, the night does seep.
Moonlight dances on leaves so bright,
Whispers of magic pierce the night.

Twinkling stars above so far,
Guide the lost with a brilliant star.
Each tree holds stories etched in bark,
In every rustle, the spirits spark.

Here in the stillness, hearts can roam,
Finding solace, a hidden home.
With every step, a world unfurls,
A midnight waltz with the unseen swirls.

Crickets serenade the hushed night air,
As shadows weave with utmost care.
In this aglow, the spirits play,
Timeless realms where dreams hold sway.

So close your eyes, let your heart feel,
An ancient magic, a vibrant reel.
In the midnight forest, free your soul,
Aglow in wonders that make you whole.

Forgotten Treasures of the Charred Glade

In the glade where the fire burned bright,
Forgotten treasures lie out of sight.
Whispers linger of stories told,
In charred remains, you'll find the gold.

Fragments of dreams in the blackened earth,
Hints of laughter, echoes of mirth.
From ashes rise, the past does speak,
Hidden gems for the brave and meek.

Nature reclaims what was once lost,
Each scar a reminder of the cost.
Yet life persists in muted hues,
In the charred glade, the spirit renews.

Beneath the soil, the roots entwine,
Holding secrets, both yours and mine.
Starlit skies watch over the glen,
In forgotten places, we start again.

So wander forth, with heart held high,
Seek the treasures that never die.
In the charred glade, where hope is stored,
Find beauty in the scars restored.

Fading Glory on the Blackened Horizon

Once vibrant skies now dimmed and gray,
Whispers of light begin to fray.
Ghostly echoes of what once was bright,
Fading glory in the depth of night.

Stars once shone with fervent glee,
Now shadows dance, wild and free.
Crimson hues merge with the black,
On this horizon, none look back.

Time has draped a velvet shroud,
Silencing dreams, the past so loud.
Hope hangs fragile in the air,
Empty promises that life laid bare.

Yet in the dark, a flicker glows,
Secrets untold, the heart still knows.
Amidst the muted tones and sighs,
Fading glory never truly dies.

So let the memories softly weave,
Into the night, we learn to believe.
A tapestry of light and shade,
On the blackened horizon, dreams are laid.

The Warmth That Survives the Scorch

Through searing heat and blistering flame,
A flicker of hope, an unquenched name.
Beneath the ashes, a heartbeat drums,
The warmth survives as darkness comes.

Charred remains of what once thrived,
Yet seeds of life are still alive.
In the furnace of despair, we find,
A strength that blooms, a heart unblind.

The sun may scorch, the winds may howl,
But from the depths, we learn to growl.
Resilience forged in trials' embrace,
The warmth that survives leaves a trace.

Through cracked foundations, we will climb,
Transcending time, a rhythm and rhyme.
For in this life, though struggles hold,
The warmth we carry cannot be cold.

So let the fire dance in our souls,
Facing the storms, we pay our tolls.
In the heart's archive, love's essence,
The warmth that thrives is our true presence.

Elegies for Fallen Luminaries

In the stillness of the starry night,
We mourn the lost, those burning bright.
Each flicker dims, a voice unheard,
Compelled by silence, we speak our word.

Luminaries fade, but not their glow,
Reflections linger, tales we sow.
In shadows cast, their legacies lie,
Elegies we craft, with every sigh.

From flickerings past, a warmth remains,
A chorus of love that never wanes.
For every star that falls from grace,
We gather light in time and space.

We raise our glasses to those who fought,
In the realm of dreams, their battles sought.
With whispered prayers and heavy hearts,
We embrace the glow that never departs.

Through ink and tears, their stories breathe,
In the chapters we write, their spirits seethe.
Elegies for fallen, yet they soar,
In ethereal skies, forevermore.

Sparks of Memory in the Gloom

In shadows deep, where silence dwells,
Sparks of memory ring like bells.
Moments flicker through the haze,
Remnants of laughter, forgotten days.

As twilight lingers, shadows play,
Echoes of voices, whisked away.
Each spark ignites a tale untold,
A treasure chest of moments bold.

In corners dark, where dreams reside,
Flickers of hope refuse to hide.
Between the lines of time's cruel tome,
Sparks of memory guide us home.

We gather fragments that fate concealed,
With gentle hands, our hearts are healed.
For in the gloom, the past can shine,
Sparks of memory, endlessly divine.

So let us cherish every trace,
Of light and love in this vast space.
In the shadows, we will bloom,
Embracing sparks of memory in the gloom.

Legends Reborn in the Ember's Embrace

In the heart of the night, legends ignite,
With whispers of glory, they soar to new heights.
Forgotten tales breathe in ember's warm glow,
Heroes arise from the ashes below.

In shadows they linger, their stories unfold,
Each spark a remembrance, each flame something bold.
Time weaves their spirit into the cool air,
Rekindled and ready, they rise without fear.

Embers dance lightly, as dreams intertwine,
A tapestry woven with threads so divine.
Voices of ancients drift soft on the breeze,
Guiding the lost ones with gentle decrees.

From flickers of darkness, the past reappears,
A symphony played on the strings of our fears.
In the glow of the night, new legends are spun,
Reborn through the warmth, as the old become one.

In ember's embrace, the tales everlast,
Reminders that time holds the future and past.
So let the flames rise, let the stories be heard,
For legends reborn shall spread wide like a bird.

Twilight's Secrets in the Blackened Wild

In twilight's soft hush, secrets take flight,
Whispers of shadows stretch into the night.
The blackened wild calls with a voice so profound,
Where mysteries linger and wonders abound.

Beneath tangled branches, the night creatures stir,
With eyes full of stories, they watch and defer.
Each rustle, each sigh, echoes deep in the dark,
As twilight reveals its hidden spark.

The moon casts a glow, pale on the ground,
Illuminating paths where lost dreams are found.
In the stillness of dusk, the unknown feels near,
A dance of the twilight, where courage meets fear.

With darkened horizons and whispers that weave,
The wild holds the truths that we dare not believe.
In the heart of the night, we breathe in the thrill,
Embracing the secrets that lie in the still.

In shadows we wander, embracing the chill,
For twilight's sweet secrets, our souls must fulfill.
Let the wildness surround, let the mysteries guide,
As the night softly drapes, with the stars open wide.

Lustrous Fragments in the Autumn Ashes

In autumn's embrace, the leaves fall like gold,
Fragments of summer, their stories retold.
With whispers of rustling on crisp, chill days,
Nature unfolds in her vibrant displays.

Amongst the bright colors, life starts to retreat,
A dance of destruction where endings meet.
Yet in every falling, there's beauty that shines,
A tapestry woven with fate's subtle lines.

The ashes of summer blend rich in the ground,
In lustrous remains, the past can be found.
Though moments may fade, their essence will stay,
A treasure of memories, come what may.

Each gust of the wind carries whispers of change,
In luster and shadows, the seasons arrange.
The warmth of the sun gives a lingering kiss,
As we cherish the fragments in autumn's abyss.

Let us gather these pieces, both bright and transcendent,
In the hearth of our hearts, they become resplendent.
In the ashes of fall, the promise is clear,
Lustrous fragments endure, forever held dear.

Shadows of Grandeur in Fallow Dreams

In the stillness of night, shadows take form,
Echoes of grandeur where hope can transform.
Fallow dreams linger, awaiting the dawn,
A tapestry woven of dusk's quiet yawn.

Whispers of visions dance lightly in air,
Past legacies linger with elegance rare.
In each fleeting moment, there's magic to find,
In shadows of grandeur, our hearts are aligned.

As stars dip their toes in the ocean of light,
Ancient tales shimmer, igniting the night.
Each breath becomes poetry, soft on the tongue,
In the depths of our being, the old songs are sung.

With time as our canvas, we paint with our fears,
Though fallow and barren, the dream still appears.
In shadows we wander, embracing our plight,
For grandeur takes root in the silence of night.

Let the echoes remind us of what we can be,
In shadows of dreams, our spirits fly free.
For even in darkness, there's brilliance to glean,
In the cradle of night, we find what we mean.

Hallowed Glow of the Withered Grove

In the hush of twilight's embrace,
Whispers dance among the trees.
Leaves rustle softly, a gentle trace,
Of memories lost on the evening breeze.

Moonlight spills on the forest floor,
Casting shadows, ethereal and pale.
Each step echoes, an ancient lore,
In this sanctum where spirits sail.

Gnarled branches reach for the sky,
With secrets held in bark and bone.
Underneath, where silence sighs,
The whispers of the past are grown.

Elders nod in a spectral light,
Guardian souls from ages past.
In their watch, the darkness takes flight,
Revealing truths that ever last.

Hallowed glow, we honor thee,
In the stillness of your grace.
Here, where time and vision weave,
We find our home, our sacred space.

Flickering Lights in the Smoky Wilderness

Beneath the veil of smoky gray,
Stars are lost in haze and gloom.
Flickering lights, they softly sway,
Guiding dreams where shadows loom.

Whispers of the wind take flight,
With secrets of the forest's heart.
Each flicker sparks in the night,
A story waiting to depart.

Embers high in the starlit sky,
Dance above the whispered trees.
They beckon wanderers who sigh,
In search of solace, peace, and ease.

Rustling leaves play a soft tune,
A lullaby for weary souls.
In the solace of the moon,
We find comfort, as night unfolds.

Wilderness holds its breath so tight,
With secrets buried deep in clay.
Flickering lights, a dying light,
Guide us gently, show the way.

Golden Reveries Beneath Ashen Canopies

In the shade of ashen boughs,
Golden dreams begin to rise.
Whispers of time, the silence vows,
To hold our hopes where twilight lies.

Beneath the canopy so grand,
Memories weave in threads of gold.
Each moment stirs like grains of sand,
In reveries that time has sold.

Gentle breezes carry sighs,
Of yesterdays we long to keep.
With every rustle, a heart replies,
In these sacred woods, we weep.

Touched by sunlight's fading glow,
The ashen leaves dance with the day.
In their embrace, we come to know,
The beauty found in dreams that sway.

Golden reveries, pure and bright,
Lead us back to where we roam.
In the ashes, find the light,
And within, we make our home.

Charcoal Dreams of Shining Legends

In the depths of night's embrace,
Charcoal dreams begin to form.
Legends whisper in this space,
Where shadows twist and spirits swarm.

Fables of the brave and bold,
Painted on the canvas vast.
Through the dark, their tales unfold,
In the echoes of the past.

Heroes rise, their voices blend,
In a chorus of time and fate.
Through the storms, they will transcend,
In the tales that resonate.

With every spark, a memory wakes,
Of battles fought and victories claimed.
In the twilight, history shakes,
As legends rise, forever named.

Charcoal dreams, they linger near,
In the heart of those who strive.
Within our souls, they live sincere,
A testament of how we thrive.

Illuminated Echoes of the Singed Boughs

In shadows deep where silence dwells,
The echoes of the past do swell.
A whispering flame, a memory's glow,
Among the boughs, the stories flow.

Charred remnants speak of what once thrived,
In the heart of darkness, new dreams arrived.
The glow of dusk, the scent of pine,
In singed remains, our hopes entwine.

Each flicker sparks, a tale untold,
In the embers lives a spirit bold.
With every breath, the night ignites,
A dance of shades, of lost delights.

Through fallen leaves where shadows loom,
We find the light midst burnt perfume.
Illuminated paths invite the wise,
To gather strength beneath the skies.

So heed the whispers, soft and low,
For every loss, a chance to grow.
In the singed boughs, life will persist,
Through illuminated echoes, we will exist.

Flickers of the Past in the Greying Woods

In twilight's haze, the woods stand still,
Whispers of history in every hill.
Old trees creak with tales of yore,
Where shadows linger, memories soar.

Flickers dance in the fading light,
Remnants of laughter in the night.
Ghostly figures move with grace,
Within the greying woods, we trace.

Each step we take stirs ancient eyes,
Beneath the boughs where silence lies.
Haunting echoes call us near,
To cherish moments once held dear.

Branches twist in a melancholic sway,
As twilight transforms the sky to gray.
The heart of night reveals its charm,
In flickers past, we find our balm.

With every rustle, a story wakes,
In the greying woods, the past remakes.
Longing whispers through the trees,
As we wander on the evening breeze.

Ethereal Lights Amongst the Burnt Remnants

Through ashes gray where silence clings,
Ethereal lights begin their flings.
A dance of hope amidst despair,
In burnt remnants, we breathe the air.

Softly glowing, the night unfolds,
Secrets buried, yet to be told.
Among the charred, new life will start,
As embered dreams ignite the heart.

Each flicker shines, a past embraced,
In ghostly hues, lost futures traced.
A tapestry spun from grief and grace,
We find our strength in this sacred space.

Amidst the ruins, spirits sing,
With every pulse, the darkness clings.
An ethereal call, a siren's plea,
Amongst the remnants, we seek to be.

So wander softly where shadows rest,
In the glow of twilight, find your quest.
Amongst the burnt, a promise awaits,
Ethereal lights to guide our fates.

Glimmers of Yesteryear in the Feral Ash

In the ashes wild where dreams ignite,
Glimmers of yesteryear spark the night.
Nature weeps for what has gone,
Yet from the grey, new hopes are drawn.

Amidst the char, a fragrance waves,
Feral tales of the life it saves.
Every flicker a gentle plea,
To remember the past and set it free.

The twilight hums with voices faint,
In nature's heart, a primal chant.
Glimmers shine through burnt terrain,
In feral ash, we bear the pain.

Let shadows weave their whispered lore,
In the silence, we find much more.
Each fleeting light, a cherished dream,
In yesteryear's glow, we find our theme.

Through wild remains, the spirit roams,
In every spark, new life finds homes.
Glimmers of what was, still to be,
In the feral ash, we shall see.

Pearls of Dawn in the Desolate Grove

In silent woods where shadows dwell,
The dawns break soft, they weave a spell.
Bright pearls of light through branches gleam,
Awakening the world from dream.

The whispers dance on gentle breeze,
Embracing vows from ancient trees.
Each dewdrop shines, a fleeting grace,
Reflecting hope in nature's face.

Beneath the boughs, secrets hide,
In every crack, in every stride.
The echoes call, a quiet tune,
Carved from the heart of morning's noon.

As sunlight spills on mossy stone,
Life's tender pulse is softly sown.
With every stir, the grove awakes,
In harmony, the forest shakes.

So linger here where silence reigns,
In beauty found, in joy, in pains.
Each pearl a dream, each spark a sigh,
In this desolate grove, we fly.

Haunted Reflections of Glorious Flames

In twilight's clutch, the embers glow,
Their whispers haunt, their shadows flow.
Reflections twirl in dusky air,
Where glorious flames dance without care.

Each flicker tells of tales long past,
Of love and loss, of shadows cast.
With every spark, a memory wakes,
As time, like smoke, forever shakes.

The night unfolds its velvet cloak,
Around the fire, in silence spoke.
Haunted eyes in flames ignite,
Seek solace in the fading light.

A ghostly waltz upon the ground,
In flickering warmth, the lost are found.
Through fiery hues, they softly tread,
In fiery dreams where hearts once bled.

With every crackle, a moment's pulse,
Of passion's rise and bitter dulled.
We sit and stare, in whispered pain,
These haunted reflections remain.

Glints of Gold in the Drifting Smoke

Amidst the haze where shadows flee,
Glints of gold set spirits free.
In drifting smoke, the visions swirl,
Like fleeting dreams in twilight's whirl.

Each shimmered light a beacon bright,
Guiding hearts through the endless night.
Whispers echo with dreams untold,
In this soft haze, the brave grow bold.

The world transforms, a canvas vast,
With strokes of beauty, shadows cast.
In smoky dreams, we search for hope,
With glints of gold, we learn to cope.

In this embrace of dusk and dawn,
Our spirit's flight forever drawn.
The drifting smoke, a veil of grace,
Where every soul finds its own place.

So let the glints of gold unfold,
In whispers soft, through stories told.
In drifting smoke, we find our way,
In every heart, a brand-new day.

Celestial Tears on the Soot-Rimmed Earth

In midnight skies, soft tears descend,
Celestial sorrows that never end.
Upon the earth, the drop leaves trace,
A soot-rimmed path, a silent space.

These tears of stars in twilight's embrace,
Fall softly down, a gentle grace.
They cleanse the world of every pain,
And in their wake, new life remains.

Each droplet holds the dreams of light,
That flickered once in endless night.
They mingle here with dust and earth,
In sorrow's song, we find rebirth.

As shadows dance in waning glow,
The tears will flow, the rivers grow.
In harmony, the heavens weep,
A lullaby for dreams to keep.

So let these tears fall on our hearts,
A sacred bond that never parts.
For in this grief, there lies the worth,
Celestial tears on soot-rimmed earth.

Vestiges of Light in the Stifled Silence

In shadows deep, whispers sigh,
Flecks of hope in a muted sky.
Faint echoes of a distant call,
Silence wraps the world in thrall.

Within the gloom, glimmers dance,
Fleeting dreams in a solemn trance.
Echoes hidden, tales untold,
Moments precious, slowly unfold.

Stars lay still, waiting to wake,
In the hush, the heart will ache.
A gentle breeze stirs the night,
Cradling warmth, a vestige of light.

The air is thick with longing sighs,
As hopes and wishes softly rise.
In stillness, shadows weave and play,
Life persists in a muted way.

Between the notes of nightingale,
In silence deep, a tender tale.
Every heartbeat, a soft glow,
In stifled silence, love will grow.

The Resplendent Remains of a Faded Past

Old stones whisper secrets vast,
Echoes linger from the past.
Time stands still in sunlit hues,
Memories dance in golden views.

Worn pathways tell of journeys gone,
In every step, a faded song.
Light and shadow sculpt the air,
Resplendence caught in moments rare.

Forgotten tales on weathered bark,
Nature holds the gentle spark.
Every crack, a story spun,
In twilight glow, their threads are run.

Through every crack, new life emerges,
In ancient roots, the heart surges.
From the dust, dreams take their flight,
Bright remains in the fading light.

In the echoes, wisdom's grace,
Time adorns with a soft embrace.
Each withered leaf is not the end,
For in the past, the heart will mend.

Glowing Heartbeats in the Burned Underbrush

Amidst the ash, new life will rise,
Through charred remains, glowing sighs.
Silent strength beneath the ground,
In the darkness, hope is found.

Flames may scorch, yet seeds will sleep,
In the soil, promises deep.
Glowing heartbeats, softly thrummed,
Resilience waits, unbound, yet numb.

Sunlight pierces, fierce and bright,
In the midst of lost delight.
Tender roots push through the fire,
Life reborn with fierce desire.

Every ember holds a spark,
This burned underbrush, a sacred park.
In the dance of flame and night,
Hope ignites with every bite.

So let the heart beat on with grace,
In the ashes, a vibrant space.
From devastation blooms the zest,
Glowing heartbeats, nature's quest.

Ashen Roots, Radiant Flowers

In twilight's hush, roots intertwine,
From ashes born, their paths align.
Beneath the soil, stories run deep,
In silent whispers, dreams will leap.

Radiant flowers break the ground,
Colors bursting all around.
From embered earth, they rise and sway,
In harmony, life's sweet ballet.

Each petal holds a glimpse of grace,
In the quiet, a warm embrace.
Ashen roots feed vibrant blooms,
In every shadow, brightness looms.

Through parched lands, the waters flow,
Nurturing life, where embers glow.
In every bud, a promise lies,
A testament to how hope flies.

So let the flowers paint the gray,
Transforming night into bright day.
For every ash, a life reborn,
Radiant flowers on a new dawn.

Forgotten Sparks Beneath the Embered Canopy

In the hush of night, whispers ignite,
Sparks dance like fireflies in the dark.
Silent secrets beneath the trees,
Memories glow, though they're stark.

Lost tales linger on the breeze,
Faded dreams wrapped in twilight's hue.
Beneath the canopy so dense,
Embers pulse, vibrant and true.

Shadows play in a gentle waltz,
Nature's heartbeat, soft and slow.
Forgotten sparks rarely fade,
They flicker in the depths below.

Among the roots where stories weave,
Each breath a promise left unspoken.
In the cool earth, life weaves,
With every spark, a heart's token.

Hope survives where darkness sprawls,
Beneath the branches, they entwine.
Lost yet found in the dusky thrall,
Forgotten sparks forever shine.

Flickering Hopes in the Charred Wilderness

In the aftermath of shadows cast,
New beginnings break the morn.
Each flicker resonates with the past,
In wilderness, hope is reborn.

Amidst the char, resilience breathes,
Tiny lights in endless night.
From ashes rise the tender leaves,
In their glow, we find our sight.

Wandering paths of soot and stone,
Soft whispers call from the void.
Flickering hopes that feel alone,
Yet, in darkness, they've deployed.

Echoes of laughter through the trees,
A reminder of days gone by.
In the stillness, we find peace,
As flickering hopes learn to fly.

As the sun dips low beneath the pines,
The wilderness hums its ancient tune.
With every spark, the heart aligns,
In the shadows, life's monsoon.

Shining Strands in a Tapestry of Ash

In the weave of twilight, gleams a thread,
Shining strands pierce the muted shades.
Dusty remnants where passions bled,
A tapestry where light cascades.

Across the canvas of the night,
Every fiber holds a dream.
In silence, stories come to light,
In the ash, whispers softly scream.

Glimmers of gold interlace the gray,
Each strand a promise, a flickering spark.
With every breath, we find our way,
In shadows deep, we leave our mark.

Fragments bright against the gloom,
In the fabric of the lost, we find.
With every thread, we weave a bloom,
Shining strands, a heart entwined.

Beneath the stars, we dance and sway,
A symphony of light and ash.
In the tapestry where memories lay,
A future bright begins to flash.

Hues of Radiance Adrift in Soot

In the depths of twilight, colors blend,
Hues of radiance softly spill.
Adrift in soot, the moments mend,
Each breath a canvas, few yet still.

Through the haze of fading light,
Shadows cradle vibrant dreams.
Whispers of day surrender night,
In darkness rich, hope loudly beams.

Brushstrokes caress the muted air,
Every hue a tale retold.
In the quiet, beauty lays bare,
Underneath the layers of cold.

As the embers quietly speak,
Colors dance in a fervent trance.
In the soot, both mild and bleak,
Hues of radiance dare to prance.

With each pulse, the darkness fades,
Adrift in colors, we're set free.
In this moment, beauty invades,
A canvas where we're meant to be.

The Snare of Glimmering Phantoms

In twilight's grasp, they softly gleam,
Phantoms dance in a silvery dream.
Whispers call from shadows near,
Enticing hearts, igniting fear.

Through tangled woods, they lead astray,
Threads of wonder, a fleeting play.
Dare to chase what you cannot see,
Lost in the web of mystery.

A flicker here, a shadow there,
Lurking phantoms, a silent snare.
In their laughter, the night takes flight,
Captivated souls, lost in delight.

Yet beware, for the path is thin,
A glittering road can lead to sin.
The deeper you fall, the further you roam,
In the snare of phantoms, you wander alone.

Luminous Portals in the Depths of Ash

Amidst the ruins, a soft glow gleams,
Portals whisper forgotten dreams.
Through ash and ember, light we find,
Awakening hearts, lost in the blind.

Ghostly echoes of ages past,
In the depths of despair, they cast.
Beneath the ashes, hope does stir,
Rising gently, a soft purr.

Open your eyes to the light within,
Let luminous portals guide you in.
Through shadows deep, we dare to tread,
Chasing the knowledge long thought dead.

In the corners of grief, there's grace,
A dance with time in a sacred space.
For every loss, a lesson bright,
In the depths of ash, a flickering light.

Shimmering Glories in Nature's Scorn

In fields of gold, the flowers sway,
Shimmering glories, come what may.
Nature's scorn cannot erase,
The beauty held in every place.

Amidst the storms and raging seas,
Resilience blooms like gentle breeze.
In chaos' grip, we find our song,
A melody of righting wrong.

With every tear that nature cries,
In the darkest nights, the starlight lies.
We stand tall, our spirits soar,
In shimmering glory, we implore.

Though shadows loom and fears may rise,
We glimpse the truth beyond the guise.
In every heart, a flame will burn,
For nature's scorn brings forth our turn.

Beacons of Brightness in the Gloomy Glade

In a glade where shadows creep,
Beacons flicker, their watch we keep.
Amidst the gloom, a spark ignites,
Guiding us through the darkest nights.

Whispers of hope on the chilling breeze,
The heart of night, still it eases.
With every step, the lanterns glow,
Uniting paths where no one goes.

Together we tread, hand in hand,
Through the shadows, we understand.
In the turning tides of fate's embrace,
We'll find our way, we'll find our place.

Beneath the branches, where dreams collide,
Beacons shine with a love that won't hide.
In the gloomy glade, we stand as one,
With brightness shared, we've just begun.

Fractured Brilliance Amongst Sooty Strands

In twilight's grasp, the shadows play,
Each flicker lost, then found astray.
Dreams adorned in tattered lace,
Whispers linger, a fragile trace.

Beneath the weight of ashen night,
Lost fragments shimmer, dim yet bright.
Echoes of laughter, long since gone,
Dance in the dark, a haunting song.

Sooty strands weave tales untold,
Of broken hearts and hopes of gold.
Through the murk, a light does gleam,
Fractured brilliance, a waking dream.

Yet in the haze, truth softly sighs,
Mirrors reflect the weary skies.
Time drips slowly, an aching muse,
Amidst the sorrow, we gently choose.

Fleeting moments etched in dust,
In fractured brilliance, we find trust.
The darkness trembles, lets us be,
Fragments of grace set wild and free.

Luminescent Ghosts of the Whispering Woods

In dense embrace, the whispers dwell,
Echoing soft like a forgotten spell.
Through ancient trees, the shadows weave,
Luminescent ghosts bid hearts believe.

Glowing softly, they beckon near,
Tales of yonder, kissed by fear.
Starlit paths beneath their gaze,
Illuminating the forgotten ways.

Mossy carpets, a gentle hue,
Frame the secrets the night winds blew.
In flickering lights, lost loves reside,
In the whispering woods, we confide.

Allure of echoes calls us forth,
To dance with visions of timeless worth.
Each breath a story, old yet new,
Beneath the moons, we wander through.

So let us roam till day awakes,
Where shadows dance and the heart breaks.
Luminescent ghosts, forever shy,
Guide us gently, till time draws nigh.

Glowing Paths in the Twilight Thicket

Twilight wraps the world in grace,
A tapestry of time and space.
Glowing paths beneath our feet,
Lead to places where dreamers meet.

In tangled thickets, secrets bloom,
Softly glowing in starlit gloom.
Each step a whisper, every sigh,
Harbors hope, while shadows lie.

Breezes carry tales untold,
Of ancient warriors and dreams unfold.
Through veils of dusk, our spirits soar,
On glowing paths, we long for more.

Faint echoes brush against the night,
As lanterns flicker, hearts take flight.
We journey forth, hand in hand,
Guided by stars, forever planned.

As dreams ignite the fading light,
In twilight thickets, all feels right.
With every heartbeat, new beginnings lie,
On glowing paths, we learn to fly.

Frayed Dreams and Glinting Shadows

In the corners of a silent room,
Frayed dreams linger, hover, loom.
Glinting shadows flicker by,
Hopes entangled, echoing sighs.

With every gesture, tales unwind,
Forgotten wishes, love entwined.
Night spills softly, moments blend,
Frayed dreams whisper, "We won't end."

In twilight's glow, our spirits gleam,
Haunted by memories, lost in a dream.
Through glinting shadows, we reside,
In broken hopes, we laugh and bide.

Each heartbeat captures a fading light,
As we cherish the ghostly night.
In every crevice, life takes flight,
Frayed dreams dance beneath the moonlight.

So let the shadows weave and spin,
For in their embrace, we begin again.
Glinting whispers, softly found,
Frayed dreams flourish all around.

Luminous Echoes Among the Ruins

In shadows deep, the whispers play,
Of ancient stone, where memories sway.
Soft beams dance on the crumbled walls,
Each echo sings as twilight calls.

Time stains the marble, yet still it gleams,
Illuminating forgotten dreams.
Ghostly figures in the fading light,
Step through the stillness of the night.

Underneath a canopy of stars,
History breathes through its silent scars.
A spectral glow on the weathered ground,
In every heartbeat, life is found.

The moonlight spills on the silent stones,
Turning the ruins into catacombs.
In this sacred dance of light and shade,
Luminous echoes serenely cascade.

To wander here is to touch the past,
Where every moment is meant to last.
In echoes soft, the stories weave,
Luminous warmth, for those who believe.

Gilded Remnants of Nature's Breath

Upon the edge of a misty dawn,
Golden leaves shimmer, quietly drawn.
Each petal whispers tales untold,
In the light's embrace, they unfold.

Beneath the boughs, time sidles slow,
Where rivers of gold in soft breezes flow.
Nature's breath caresses each tree,
In gilded remnants, wild and free.

The rustling grass sings praises sweet,
A chorus where earth and sky meet.
Sunbeams linger on dew-soaked ground,
Woven with magic, serenity found.

Amidst the thorns, wildflowers bloom,
Transforming the shadows, dispelling gloom.
With every sunrise, hope is reborn,
In gilded remnants, the heart is worn.

Let the breeze carry whispers of light,
As day surrenders to the coming night.
In nature's arms, we come alive,
In gilded remnants, together we thrive.

Radiant Spirits Amidst the Scorched Foliage

In a world where fire kissed the ground,
Shadows linger, where warmth was found.
Amidst the ashes, spirits rise,
Radiant glimmers beneath the skies.

With every ember, stories ignite,
Of battles fought in the dark of night.
The foliage scorched, yet life holds on,
In radiant spirits, resilience drawn.

Through charred remains, new life will grow,
From loss and pain, beauty will show.
In the flicker of flames, a promise sways,
Radiant spirits dance in wild displays.

With hope reborn in the fragrant air,
Nature whispers secrets with tender care.
Against the scars, the heart must strive,
For radiant spirits will always thrive.

So let us walk among these trees,
Where light and shadow intertwine with ease.
In every flicker, we'll find our way,
Radiant spirits, forever stay.

Fragments of Brilliance in the Twilight

As day concedes to the night's embrace,
Fragments of brilliance begin to trace.
In the twilight hue, the stars ignite,
A dance of colors, a fleeting sight.

The horizon blushes with tender light,
Casting dreams as day takes flight.
Soft whispers echo on the gentle breeze,
In fragments of brilliance, hearts find ease.

Misty shadows weave tales once told,
In shimmering fabrics of red and gold.
Each moment captured, a fleeting glance,
In twilight's glow, a serene dance.

The moon ascends, a silvered crest,
Bathing the world in its gentle rest.
Fragments of brilliance in the dim,
An ethereal song on the wind's whim.

Let us wander in this twilight dream,
Where every flicker is more than it seems.
In these transient moments, forever find,
Fragments of brilliance, two souls aligned.

Glistening Memories of the Burned Vale

In the vale where shadows play,
Sparks of laughter softly sway,
Echoes of a brighter time,
Glistening in the morning prime.

Amid the charred and brittle tree,
Memories of you and me,
Winds that whisper through the pines,
Bringing forth the lost designs.

Flowers bloom from ashes gray,
Hope reborn in a new day,
Beneath the sky, a canvas bright,
Glistening dreams take their flight.

Through the smoke and burning haze,
We recount those golden days,
In the vale, our spirits thrive,
Glistening tales of love alive.

Every corner holds a spark,
Guiding us through endless dark,
With every breath, the past remains,
In the vale, love never wanes.

Faded Stars in the Ashen Night

Faded stars in evening's breath,
Whispers of a beauty, death,
In the dark, the embers sigh,
Asking questions, asking why.

Shadows dance on memories lost,
Each heartbeat counts the cost,
In the silence, stories fade,
As the velvet sky cascades.

Once they sparkled, shining bright,
Guided sailors through the night,
Now they flicker, dimmed by ash,
Echoes bound in a fleeting flash.

With each glance, I long to see,
The light that once set us free,
Scaled by time, the stars remain,
Faded dreams, a lingering pain.

In the ashes, hope is sewn,
From the darkness, seeds are grown,
A cosmic dance of loss and gain,
Faded stars, forgotten pain.

Gilded Whispers Beneath the Soot

Amidst the ruins, silence spreads,
Gilded whispers, soft as threads,
Underneath the soot and grime,
Echoes linger, lost in time.

Each layer hides a story told,
Secrets wrapped in hearts of gold,
In the shadows, memories weave,
Beneath the soot, we still believe.

Fingers trace the paths of years,
Through the dust, the joy, the tears,
Every sigh a gentle clue,
Gilded whispers calling you.

With each breath, the past ignites,
Carried on the winds of nights,
In the quiet, sparks ignite,
Gilded echoes take their flight.

From the ashes, dreams ascend,
Flickering hopes, time's loyal friend,
In the soot, we find our truth,
Gilded whispers of our youth.

Glance of Gold on Charcoaled Landscapes

In the dawn of a new embrace,
A glance of gold across the space,
Charcoaled landscapes, stark and bare,
Awakening dreams to breathe the air.

Sunrise paints a hopeful scene,
Every shadow wears a sheen,
Fires of yesterday now cool,
Gold glimmers, breaking every rule.

From the ruins, life starts anew,
Nature's canvas drenched in hue,
In the glow, the past retreats,
Gold entwined where sorrow meets.

Every step, a gentle trace,
Guiding through this hallowed space,
Charcoal trails and rays unite,
In the gold, we find our light.

As we walk through ashes gray,
Hope ignites, and fears give way,
With a glance, the heart can see,
Gold's embrace, our legacy.

Shattered Splendor Amongst the Darkened Boughs

In shadows deep, where whispers glide,
Faded dreams in silence hide.
The boughs, once grand, now twisted low,
Bear the weight of grief and woe.

Crimson leaves in chaos sway,
Tales of light that went astray.
Yet through the cracks, a glow can start,
A flicker of the yearning heart.

Echoes of laughter, soft and fleet,
Rustling softly 'neath the feet.
Memories linger, ghosts of grace,
In this realm, they find their place.

Beneath the gloom, the roots entwine,
Binding stories, lost and divine.
Each splintered branch, a tale to tell,
Of beauty marred, yet love's farewell.

So in the dark, we search and yearn,
For splendor's light, a way to learn.
From shattered dreams, new paths arise,
Amongst the dark, hope's ember flies.

Celestial Whispers in the Wasted Woods

Beneath the canopy, shadows roam,
In silent groves, they find a home.
Stars above weave tales of old,
In gentle winds, their truths unfold.

Trees stand tall, their stories bare,
Whispers drift through the cool night air.
In every rustle, there's a song,
A reminder that we all belong.

The moonlight bathes the forest floor,
In silver shimmers, we explore.
Celestial secrets guide our feet,
Through winding paths, the heart's own beat.

Nature's breath, a soothing sound,
In wasted woods, peace can be found.
Amongst the ruins, life will grow,
With every spirit, dreams will flow.

Through the darkness, we see the light,
In whispers soft, we take our flight.
Celestial gifts, in silence bound,
In the wasted woods, we are found.

Wreathed in Ashes, Yet Shining Still

In the wake of embers, shadows lie,
Years of history whispering by.
Ashes fall like memories spent,
A testament to what was meant.

Yet in the soot, a glimmer gleams,
Flickers of hope, like ancient dreams.
From charred remains, new life can rise,
Wreathed in ashes, the spirit flies.

Through bitter trails, the heart does seek,
In the husk of silence, it learns to speak.
Though fire raged, and darkness cast,
The soul endures, the die is cast.

With every step on hollow ground,
Resilience blooms where pain is found.
Through the rubble, a strength revealed,
Wreathed in ashes, the heart is healed.

So lift the veil of night's despair,
Find the beauty hidden there.
In every scar, a lesson instilled,
Wreathed in ashes, yet shining still.

Flickers of Hope in the Cinder Fields

In fields of cinders, where embers sleep,
The night's cool breath begins to creep.
Barren land with tales untold,
Yet flickers dance, both brave and bold.

Against the gray, a spark ignites,
A rallying cry for the weary nights.
In every corner, shadows coalesce,
Yet hope arises, bright and blessed.

Among the ruins, hearts do wander,
In search of dreams, of light to ponder.
Each step a promise, each breath a fight,
In cinder fields, we chase the light.

The sun will rise, with colors bright,
To paint the sky with warmth and might.
Flickers grow into flames anew,
In every heart, a path to pursue.

So linger not where darkness reigns,
For in the ashes, love sustains.
From cinder fields, we take our stand,
Flickers of hope, a guiding hand.

Sparkling Tales from the Faded Wilderness

In whispers soft, the trees recount,
The tales of life on a rugged mount.
Stars above in the night do gleam,
Lighting dreams that once did seem.

The rivers dance, with laughter bright,
In shadows deep, they seek the light.
Each pebble holds a story true,
Of love once lost and hopes anew.

Among the petals, fragrances drift,
In nature's arms, the spirits lift.
The echoes call, a sweet embrace,
Inviting all to join the chase.

With every breeze, the memories swell,
Of moments caught in a wishing well.
Where dreams can soar like birds in flight,
In sparkling tales, all hearts unite.

Through wildflowers and tangled vines,
The heartbeat of the earth aligns.
With vibrant hues, the stories bloom,
In faded wilderness, there's room.

Glowing Relics in the Silence of Ash

Amidst the ruins, whispers rise,
Of glowing relics 'neath darkened skies.
In ashes cold, warm embers survive,
Tales unspoken, yet still alive.

The memories linger, a haunting grace,
In every corner, a forgotten space.
Where silence speaks in hushed refrain,
Of hopes and dreams, both lost and gained.

As shadows dance, the past awakes,
In flickers bright, the heart can quake.
Through ancient halls, the spirits roam,
In this stillness, they find their home.

Each echo tells of battles fought,
In every stone, a lesson taught.
From glowing relics, wisdom springs,
In the silence of ash, the future sings.

In fading light, the stories call,
Of love that rises, through every fall.
With every heartbeat, the night unfolds,
In glowing relics, the truth beholds.

Illuminated Spirits Amongst the Blight

Beneath the weight of sorrowed skies,
Illuminated spirits rise and fly.
Amidst the blight, they find their song,
In shadows deep, where they belong.

Among the thorns, a light does creep,
In solitude, their secrets keep.
With whispered hopes, they weave the night,
Guiding lost souls with gentle light.

Through battered paths, their whispers lead,
With every step, a stronger creed.
Yet in the dark, they shine so bright,
Illuminating wrong with right.

The blight may come, but they remain,
In every sorrow, there's joy to gain.
With flickering flames, they turn the tide,
In illuminated hearts, love will bide.

Through troubled times, they weave their fate,
In every heart, they navigate.
A tapestry of light and night,
Amongst the blight, they find their flight.

Resilient Gleams Amidst the Darkened Thicket

In thickets dense where shadows play,
Resilient gleams shall light the way.
With every thorn, a story weaves,
Of strength reborn in winter leaves.

The tangled roots, a steadfast hold,
In nature's arms, such tales unfold.
Through trials fierce, the heart beats strong,
In darkened thickets, where it belongs.

Each whispered breeze, a soothing balm,
Amidst the chaos, the spirit's calm.
With eyes aglow, they rise anew,
In resilient hearts, the dreamers grew.

Though shadows loom and fears surround,
In every heartbeat, hope is found.
With radiant light, they push the night,
Resilient gleams, forever bright.

Through tangled paths and winding trails,
The essence of life forever prevails.
In every struggle, a lesson shines,
Amidst the darkened thicket, love aligns.

Echoes of Glory in the Embered Wilds

In twilight's grip, shadows wane,
Whispers of past, a soft refrain.
Amongst the pines, the embers glow,
A dance of fire, a tale of woe.

Each crackle sings of dreams long lost,
A testament to the tempest's cost.
Through every spark, a story breathes,
In the wild's heart, the spirit weaves.

Beneath the stars, the night expands,
Memory's touch on sable sands.
With every flame, the echoes cry,
Of battles fought, beneath the sky.

In silence deep, the woods reside,
Where courage and despair abide.
Through embered trails, the past will call,
In every shadow, we stand tall.

With every rustle in the leaves,
History whispers, hope receives.
In the glow, a promise shines,
That from the ashes, strength aligns.

So let the wilds remember true,
The echoes of a life anew.
For in the dark, a spark remains,
Glory reflected in reverent veins.

Glinting Spirits in the Smoky Depths

In the fog's embrace, shadows play,
Spirits linger where light will sway.
Glimmers dance in twilight's fall,
A haunting song, a siren's call.

Through tendrils of smoke, whispers hide,
Silence folds where secrets bide.
Each flicker tells a tale untold,
Of dreams once bright, now faintly bold.

In smoky depths, the echoes sigh,
A tapestry of life gone by.
Beneath the veil, the past resides,
With every breath, the hope abides.

Ethereal hues in waning light,
Guide the lost through endless night.
In the shadows, spirits gleam,
As daylight fades, they softly dream.

With every heartbeat, tales revive,
In smoky depths, the lost survive.
Their glinting forms, a beacon bright,
Illuminate the path of night.

Twinkling Dreams Amidst the Charcoal Veil

Amidst the ash, a whisper glows,
A flicker born where it softly flows.
Twinkling dreams in charcoal's breath,
Defy the shadows, conquer death.

In midnight's haze, the wishes soar,
To distant realms, forevermore.
Each spark a wish, a fleeting flight,
A promise made beneath the night.

In quiet reverie, hearts ignite,
Yearning for the spark of light.
The charcoal veil, a canvas drear,
Yet in its depths, our dreams appear.

Through the darkness, hope entwines,
We carve our fate through endless signs.
Twinkling hearts, we dwell within,
The flame of life, undimmed by sin.

So let the embers guide our way,
Through twilight's gloom and dawning ray.
In charred remains, our dreams take flight,
Embracing all that feels so right.

The Golden Remnants of a Scorched Landscape

In fields of gold where ashes lay,
The sun breaks forth to greet the day.
Scorched remains breathe life anew,
With every seed, the earth breaks through.

Golden remnants of battles fought,
In every grain, a lesson taught.
From fire's wrath, resilience born,
A vibrant bloom, a brand new morn.

As nature weeps, it also sings,
Of healing's touch and gentle springs.
The landscape bears a scarred embrace,
Yet finds its grace in time and space.

Through golden light, the shadows fade,
In every corner where dreams are laid.
A testament to survival's grace,
The scorched earth finds its rightful place.

In the remnants, hope will glean,
A future bright, a world serene.
Through every trial, love prevails,
In the golden light, the heart unveils.

Dreams of Radiance in Singed Borders

In fractured skies where shadows blend,
Flickers of hope through darkness send.
A whispering light aglow in flight,
Awakes the heart, ignites the night.

Each ember's glow a distant star,
Guiding lost souls from afar.
Through burning dreams, we find our way,
To brighter worlds where we can stay.

Amidst the ashes, colors bloom,
Softening edges of despair's gloom.
We dance on pathways forged by pain,
Our spirits rise, we break the chain.

With each scar worn, a tale to tell,
Of battles fought, of rising swell.
In singed borders, courage thrives,
Where dreams take root and hope survives.

A tapestry woven from the fire,
In radiant hues, we all conspire.
Embrace the light, let darkness yield,
In dreams of radiance, hearts are healed.

Lustrous Visions in the Embers' Wake

In the hush of night, embers glow,
Tales of the past in whispers flow.
Visions emerge from the fading light,
Wrapped in the warmth of tender night.

Ghostly figures dance in grace,
In lustrous dreams, they find their place.
Fields of starlight, skies of flame,
Remind us all, we are the same.

Through the smoke, a path is drawn,
Not lost, but reborn at dawn.
In tender moments, memories stray,
Lush visions bloom in embers' play.

Shadows linger where fires fade,
In this twilight, dreams are made.
With every flicker, courage wakes,
New worlds arise in sudden breaks.

So close your eyes, let visions flow,
In the embers' wake, let spirit grow.
Embrace the light that memory sows,
In lustrous dreams, the heart bestows.

Shining Memories Amidst the Decay

In ruins deep where echoes lie,
Memories shine, they never die.
Amongst the dust, the past unfolds,
In shimmering light, a story holds.

What once was lost is found anew,
In every glimpse, a vibrant hue.
Amidst decay, the beauty thrives,
In shining hope, the heart survives.

Glimmers of joy through sorrow seep,
In fractured time, our spirits leap.
We gather the fragments, piece by piece,
In golden warmth, we find release.

The laughter shared, the tears we've shed,
In tangled roots, our passions spread.
A tapestry rich, with colors bold,
In shining memories, life unfolds.

So when the world feels cold and bare,
Remember the light that lingers there.
For in the ruins, life will play,
In shining memories, we find our way.

Essence of Dawn in the Charred Jungle

In charred remains where silence speaks,
The essence of dawn gently creeps.
Through broken branches, light will roam,
Awakening life to its new home.

A canvas painted with shades of gray,
Yet hope emerges in the fray.
In every scar, a tale is spun,
In the jungle's heart, a new day begun.

With each soft breath, the forest sighs,
As whispers dance in the morning skies.
The essence of dawn, so pure, so bright,
Guides weary souls back to the light.

Beneath the ashes, seeds are sown,
From charred remains, resilience grown.
In nature's arms, despair we'll see,
Transforming into wild jubilee.

So cherish the dawn, let shadows fade,
In the charred jungle, dreams are made.
For from the ruins, life will stand,
In the essence of dawn, hand in hand.

www.ingramcontent.com/pod-product-compliance
Ingram Content Group UK Ltd.
Pitfield, Milton Keynes, MK11 3LW, UK
UKHW021538210125
4208UKWH00025B/713